Facing
CHALLENGES
IN THE
LAND OF SMILES

EMILIE MARGARET BALLARD

FACING CHALLENGES IN THE LAND OF SMILES

Scripture quotations are taken from the Holy Bible, New International Version®, NIV®. Copyright © 1973, 1978, 1984 by Biblica, Inc.™ Used by permission of Zondervan. All rights reserved worldwide.

iUniverse books may be ordered through booksellers or by contacting:

iUniverse
1663 Liberty Drive
Bloomington, IN 47403
www.iuniverse.com
844-349-9409

ISBN: 978-1-6632-4017-0 (sc)
ISBN: 978-1-6632-4018-7 (e)

Print information available on the last page.

iUniverse rev. date: 06/21/2022

PREFACE

God has blessed me richly throughout my long life. For some years I have thought that eventually I would write up my memoirs. That is why I saved all the letters, manuscripts, and photos that might be useful when the time finally came to do so. I envisioned three or four volumes. Book I, about my family background, and my life and experiences during my first thirty-nine years of life, has already been published. It ended with my appointment as a missionary to work with the Karen people of Burma. My Book II is about my work and experiences in Burma, now called Myanmar. It also has already been published. Book III is about my work and experiences in Thailand. Book IV would be about my experiences since retirement. Of course, much depends on whether God chooses to let me live long enough to complete all of these or not.

I am grateful to my father for saving all of my letters to him from childhood on, making this book possible. I started this book towards in the middle of 2019 with the hope of publishing it by the middle of 2020. However, I was not able to due to the pandemic. As stated in Jeremiah 29:11 11, "For I know the plans I have for you," declares the LORD, "plans **to prosper** you and not to harm you, plans to give **you** hope and a future." I thank God for His wonderful plan.

INTRODUCTION

A. The 4 verses of the hymn "How Firm a Foundation" fit the 4 stages of my life. the first verse describes my childhood and pre-missionary days; the second verse describes my experiences in Burma (now called Myanmar); the third verse describes my experiences in Thailand; and the fourth verse describes my retirement years.

The third verse says:

"When through fiery trials thy pathway shall lie,
My grace, all sufficient, shall be thy supply.
The flame shall not hurt thee; I only design.
Thy dross to consume and thy gold to refine.

The Fiery Trials in the third verse (i.e., The main challenges there were:)

1) Relationship with mission colleagues and national co-workers from various national cultural and religious backgrounds
2) The study of the "Thai" language in the Union Language School
3) Difficulties of travel and of getting financial support.
4) Problems of administration
5) Surgical and medical problems
6) Adapting to the climate and seasons
7) Car accidents

8) Relocation made necessary because of the government's damming the rivers to get hydroelectric power.
9) Murders and attempted murders
10) Revolt of the teaching staff

The challenges were not faced by me alone, but by many others as well. But in them I can see that for me at least, they have forced me to pray more and seek the Lord's guidance more earnestly and to realize more and more how God was using them to "consume the dross and refine the gold" in my life.

B. Why Thailand Is called the 'Land of Smiles'

Asia had become one of the biggest tourist destinations in the world, whether the continent was ready for it or not. Some countries were slow and more cautious to jump at the chance to please the herds of tourists flying in from Milan to Miami, however, Thailand saw its opportunity in the industry and tailored itself as such. Thus, the Land of Smiles was born.

The nickname was first dubbed in a promotional sense, hoping to lure visitors in with its promise of white sand beaches, affordable travel costs, and the extreme hospitality of the locals. This, in a sense, was all very realistic. The coastlines of Southern Thailand are some of the most stunning in the world. The cost of accommodation and food remained extremely low in comparison to Western countries and even those surrounding the Land of Smiles. Last but not least, the locals were, for the most part, helpful, courteous, and kind.

It was this nickname that explained most of the country's brochures: a smiling local selling goods at a floating market or similar. That being said, this same market was likely swarming with tourists … though the photograph does not show it. Thailand welcomed some 32 million foreign tourists in the year 2018, and the country's momentum in terms of visitors did not seem to be slowing down.

Another reason why the country may have gained this nickname was because Thai people really did smile, or *yim*, a lot, even in situations where a smile was not always warranted. Saving face was important to many Thais. Instead of showing an emotion like anger or anxiety, for example, some locals would simply slap on a smile and act as if all was well. While this might have been a relief to some visitors who expected the Land of Smiles to fulfill its inherent nickname, others might find the smiling front confusing.

I

NEW ASSIGNMENT

A. After being forced to leave Burma (now called Myanmar), I spent several months doing deputation talking about the work in that country. I had been assigned to work with the Pwo Karen tribe in the vicinity of Sangkla on one of the 3 streams emptying into the Little River Kwai. Sangkla is opposite a point about mid-way between Moulmein and Tavoy. The border land is quite mountainous and Sangkla is in the foothills. In addition to the Pwo Karen ethnic group, there were also Thai and Mon villages.

This mission project was a joint project with a Disciples Mission and was about 5 miles from the 3 Pagodas Pass. The Disciples Mission provided a doctor, whose wife was the nurse in charge of the nursing side of the hospital. When I visited there while on vacation from language school, there was a 10-bed hospital, and villagers were coming for medical care.

The Pwo Karens in that area were mostly illiterate. They were mostly animists, i.e., spirit worshipers. They were at least one hundred years behind the Karens of the Bassein-Myaungmya area in Burma where I had worked before.

B. Preparation for New Assignment

In preparation for the new assignment, I took a 5-month literacy course at the Koinonia Foundation near Baltimore. This foundation was

1

started after World War II by 12 men of prayer, including Dr. Frank Labauch and Starr Daily, a spiritual training center for a Christian person expecting to go overseas in government service, foreign-aid programs, or in business. The purpose was that they might be better able to be channels of God's love, joy, and power in other lands. Later, Dr. Labauch persuaded the foundation to add literacy training as well.

After completing the course, I returned to the home of my aunt and uncle in Rockport, Texas, to get my needed articles bought and shipped to the West Coast. Then I went to southern California for a short visit before going on to San Francisco to sail.

C. Trip to Thailand

God works everything perfectly in every detail. For example, there were about 20 missionaries on board the ship, and we had good fellowship together, strengthening one another in prayer and witnessing. Then, God arranged for us to visit the Vacation Bible School at Pearl Harbor on the other side of the island of Honolulu. We had fellowship at lunch time with the pastor and once again at supper time with the church family. The weather was warm all the way, and there was no rough weather. There were about 2 brief squalls that lasted about 30 minutes each. A typhoon was predicted the day before we arrived at Hong Kong, but it was delayed until the ship had docked, and we had reached our hotel.

We had a pleasant 3 days in Hong Kong, including attending a Chinese dinner given in honor of the arrival of the Schocks (former Burma Missionaries) who had been re-assigned to Hong Kong. The Loren Norens also had returned from furlough (home leave) about a week before we got there, and it was good to see them also.

II

ARRIVAL IN THAILAND

A. I flew from Hong Kong to Bangkok, arriving about 4 pm on August 25. Because the Baptist Missionary Conference was being held down at the YWCA camp site on the ocean about a 3-hour trip from Bangkok, I was whisked down there the same evening. I got in on the last 2-1/2 days of the conference. Because of my previous trips to Thailand, I knew about half of the missionaries there, and had met some of the others once.

You would never guess where I was staying. I was in half of a duplex owned by a princess! She was the great granddaughter of the King referred to in "The King and I". We were on the same telephone line as her family. Sometimes, someone would call and ask if the "Royal Highness" was there. The house was in a large compound containing 3 houses altogether. There were 4 or 5 ponds that were stocked with fish that were raised as pets. There were also beautiful trees and shrubberies there. It was quiet and peaceful, yet with easy access to the buses and shops. The princess lived in the other half of the duplex and rented this half to our Mission for the single women missionaries. She designed it herself and it was beautiful! Really, it didn't seem like "missionary quarters" at all; but because the Mission could assure her that there would be no children, and no carousing at night, and that the house and furniture would be taken good care of, she was persuaded to rent it to us for a reasonable fee. This was just another evidence of God's loving provision for our needs!

B. Language School

1. I really enjoyed language school, even though we had to work hard. It was such a joy to be able to study in a class with other students (mostly missionaries). A well worthwhile course taught by teachers who were experienced in teaching Westerners, who knew how to drill us, and who were there to correct us. In Burma, there were not enough missionaries learning the language at the same time to make it feasible to have a language school.

2. We were allowed to take up to 2 hours a week of outside responsibility if we wished. So, I began teaching English 2 nights a week to a group of young people at the Community Christian Center (one of the mission projects among the Chinese). The members of the center church were mostly young people. For the majority of them, the first point of contact with Christians was through the English classes. I usually attended the morning service on Sunday mornings. That not only gave me a chance to fellowship with the fine young church members there but also become familiar with the Thai religious language, since the Chinese young people used Thai more than Chinese.

3. In the evenings, I usually attended the English service at the International Church, which was inter-denominational, where I could really understand. It also afforded me an opportunity to meet other American Christians besides our Baptist missionaries. Once a month there was a church fellowship supper and meeting, which also gave a better opportunity for getting acquainted. I was also blessed with a prayer-mate with whom I met every Saturday morning. She was with the Child Evangelism Fellowship.

4. Every 2 months I had to leave Thailand because of my temporary visa. The mission paid my way to the nearest safe place, and if we went farther, we had to pay the difference ourselves. But, during the Christmas holiday, birthday and Christmas gifts enabled me to stop in Burma for 24 hours on the way to Calcutta and the way back to Thailand. Mrs. Louise Paw hosted me, and I got to see many friends during my 2 trips.

C. Mission Work, Challenges, and Good Things

1. Many folks were praying for me, and my ministry and God was moving in wonderful ways to accomplish his purposes. For example: there was a Thai man named Prawat. He was a chronic tuberculosis patient and an Opium addict at the hospital. He found the Lord and then began reading God's Word, which gave him increasing spiritual strength. He was not very well physically. Another example of God's working was seeing a Pwo Karen's boy in his early twenties, who went to Chiang Mai in the northern part of Thailand, to the Center for the uplift of the Hill Tribes. He was the first native of Sangkla to find the Lord, and his parents were against it. He was one of the protégés of a part-time evangelist named Mary. In spite of Mary's declining physical health, God continued to use her witness as long as she lived, and many other young people found the Lord as their savior as a result.

2. In Bongti Village, which was a Sgaw Karen village quite far from the rest of our work, there was evidence that the Holy Spirit was definitely working. A young evangelist and his wife had been working there for about two years. One or two persons were backslidden Christians, and the rest were all Buddhists. The school principal, his two teen-age children, and his younger brother, who was married to a backslidden Christian, all asked for baptism. They were under instruction. Judging from the interest and enthusiasm of some of the others. Before long they also took a stand for Christ.

Karens loved to sing, and there were so many villagers in the choir that the evangelist's house couldn't hold them all during rehearsals, so some had to stand on the ground below and sing. (The house was on stilts raising it about four feet from the ground.) were so many villagers in the choir that the evangelist's house couldn't hold them all during rehearsals, so some had to stand on the ground below and sing. (The house was on stilts raising it about four feet from the ground.) The house was on stilts raising it about 4 feet from the ground. So, some of the choir members had to stand on the ground to sing during rehearsal. The following Christmas he took the choir on a 3-day singing tour of the surrounding Christian villages.

The villagers gave gifts amounting to more than 600 bahts, (equivalent to about $50.) The tour used a small portion of it for gifts for the children, and prizes for the Christmas sports competitions. But most of it was used to buy a kerosene pressure lamb to replace the usual tiny kerosene lamps. The people carried when they went out at night.

For their three-day Christmas celebration, they pooled their resources and energy to feed free of charge some 80 villagers from the three Christian villages where they had gone to sing. On the last evening one of them said, "Always before when we did anything as a village project, we got drunk; and usually there have been several brawls. But this time we had drunk only tea, and yet we enjoyed ourselves."

I took the Government nursing examination the first week of February and passed it. It was something like the State Board examinations in America, though not so difficult. I could not practice as a nurse in Thailand until I had passed the examination.

Our Thailand Mission published an 8-page mimeographed newssheet called the Thailand Tatler, which included news and reports of the association work and also photographs.

I finally arrived at the mission station of Sangkla. It was beautiful there, so much of God's beautiful creation all around to enjoy and to remind one of His power and providence! I could see two bends of the river from my house, some mountains in the background, and many, many lovely trees and shrubs as well as many kinds of birds and butterflies.

There were many Pwo Karen, Mon, Burman, and Thai villages in the area, and we had patients of all four tribes in our hospital at one time or another; so often the doctor had to use a member of the staff as an interpreter. Fortunately, all four tribes were also represented on the hospital staff. The villages were all small, and most of the people had very little education. They were mostly quite poor, and although I thought otherwise before I got here, I found that they were mostly Buddhist. Resistance to Christianity was strong. Satan was also very evidently determined to do all he could to prevent the Lord's work from going forward. However, I believed in the power of God to carry out His purpose, and it was plainly His purpose to have those people know that He loved them and had provided for their salvation.

The Mission station had a 10-bed hospital; a school with classes from kindergarten through the 4th-grade, with an enrollment of about 80 pupils. There was a Thai evangelist there and Karen's evangelists in three other villages. The work was only about seven years old, and up to that time, only four persons, other than children of Christian workers, had accepted Christ.

The community in which I lived, Sangkla, was also the name of the district, which was equivalent to a state and was also the name of the capital town. The name "River Kwai" brought to the average western mind a particular river because of the book and the movie by that name. However, the word "kwai," actually means "river," and hence does not refer to any particular one to the Thai. The real name of the "River Kwai" is "Kwai Noi" – (The "ai" is pronounced as a short "a" as in "bad" and the second word is pronounced "naw-wee" with the voice rising on the last syllable in a questioning tone of voice.) The inflection of the voice was very important in Thai. If one used the wrong inflection, the meaning became something different. Our Kwai River Christian Mission (KRCM) was not actually on the Kwai Noi, but on one of the three streams which join to form that body of water (see map).

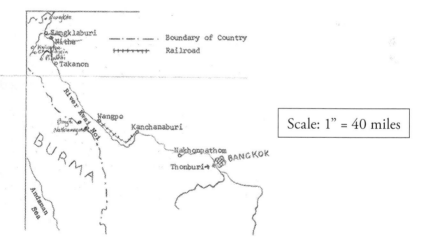

I spent much of the next two months in language study, as the dialect of Pwo Karen spoken there was different from that which I had used in Burma. After that I did quite a bit of traveling out to the villages to get the lay of the land, get acquainted with the villagers, and to witness as the opportunity arose. I also helped with the religious program of the hospital and helped set up Thai language lessons for the nurses. They were from Burma and didn't yet know Thai. There was one teenage girl in the village who wanted to become a Christian, and whose grandmother sent her there to stay with a Christian family so that she could learn the Christian way. The lab technician at the hospital also claimed to be a secret believer but was afraid to take a stand for Christ publicly because his wife was a strong Buddhist. I started classes for these two people soon to teach them the way of salvation and the basic beliefs of Christianity.

The map shows where I was in relation to Bangkok. The usual way of travel was by bus or taxi from Bangkok to Kanchanaburi (Kanburi, for short) (depending upon how much stuff we had to take with us), from there we took the train to Wangpo, then by jet-propelled motorboat the rest of the way to Nithe˚ (nee-tay), the name of the village where we lived. It was 14-hour trip going down river, but 1 1/2 days coming upriver because we stayed overnight at Kanburi. (It couldn't easily be done in one day coming up). In the dry season we could come up by boat only to Takonon and had to go the rest of the way by land rover over a very bad road.

Up to that time, our home mission workers had all been supported by gifts from the USA as we did not yet have any local churches in that area. That January at the annual meeting of the Thailand Baptist Convention, composed mainly of Christian Karens and Lahus in the northwestern part of Thailand, a young Bible School graduate was dedicated as a missionary to the Sangkla Mission. He was the Convention's first missionary to be sent away from the districts covered by the Convention, and he would be supported partly by the Convention and partly by the alumni of the Bible School.

It became evident last July that it would be necessary to close the hospital when the doctor would be returning to his country, we didn't know what arrangements to make for Prawat. He was too sick to travel very far, and as he was far from home, he had no friends or relatives nearby who could look after him. We prayed about it, and the Lord solved the problem by calling him to be with Him – quietly during Prawat's sleep about ten days before the hospital closed. Although he didn't have the opportunity to be baptized, he loved the Bible and read it often during the day.

The boy, *David* completed his first year in the Bible School at the Center for the Uplift of the Hill Tribes near Chiang Mai and returned to Sangkla to do his field work. So, he and the Karen missionary sent by TKBC (Thailand Karen Baptist Convention), spent about six weeks visiting the Pwo Karen villages in the area giving their testimonies and talking with the villagers about Christ. The reports which they gave us at the end of their trip enabled us to know better what the attitude of the people in each of these villages was toward Christianity, and which places gave evidence that follow-up work would be of value.

Two other young people from Sangkla were baptized before the end of the year after a period of instruction. One is a young man named Chatri, who had the chance last year to enter our fine Christian high school at Bang Saen. His mother was a strong Buddhist and did not want him to become a Christian at all. But ever since December he kept begging her to allow him to be baptized. When she was finally convinced that nobody was pressuring him, but that it was his own desire and decision, she at last gave permission.

The other one who had asked for baptism was a teen-age girl named *Naw Mu,* who was an orphan adopted by one of our Christian workers. Her uncle had warned her since she was quite young that under no circumstances was, she ever to become a Christian. However, she finally persuaded her uncle to allow her to be baptized.

Our hope here was mainly in these young people with whom we had been able to work since their childhood. I could not help believing that there were other young people, also who were thinking about accepting Christ. Soon after school opened on May 18, I opened an instruction class and invited all who were interested to come.

A woman in a village in the Bikhi area also requested baptism. She was blamed by the villagers for causing an evil spirit to enter certain persons and make them sick – at least the divination points to her as the culprit. She, herself, was helpless to do anything about it, and was afraid both of the spirits and of the villagers who might decide to kill her. Having heard from the home mission worker of how Jesus had power over the evil spirits, she wanted to become a Christian. The day after she convinced the worker that she really meant it, the worker had to leave for the annual meeting of the Thailand Baptist Convention followed by an evangelistic trip, and she had just gotten back.

Although Bongti village was quite far from us, it was still connected with our Sangkla Mission. This previous Christmas the first four villagers had been baptized, and another three the week after Easter. Ten others attended the instruction classes and were baptized that Christmas. Two of the new converts entered Bible School the following year in April. All of them met together and formally organized a church. The spirit of the whole village changed tremendously during the three years that the young couple were working there. Before long, the whole village accepted Christ. Then a village about half a day's walk away from them asked for a worker to teach them the way.

Following the Thailand Baptist Convention's annual meeting, some of our workers and young people accompanied me to the various villages where we had heard wanted to have Christians visit them.

The young man, Chatri, was baptized on January 16th at the Sammuk Christian Academy, where he had been studying. Three villagers from Bongti Village, including the school principal and his wife, were baptized on January 2nd, along with two young people from the nearby village of Nonh-si-monkhon where we had started work. Three of these five persons planned to go to Bible School in May. Two who were baptized last Easter had completed their first year in Bible School, so we were greatly encouraged and anticipated further evidence of the Holy Spirit's working.

We began a work in Pilokki (Bee-law-kee) Village, where we had found three backslidden Christians who wanted to return to the Lord. There were also three who had had some contact with Christians and wanted to follow Christ. And at Laykawtee Village, just 1 1/2 hours' walk away, there were several others who were interested.

I was very happy that a new missionary family came to help with the work at Sangkla – the Edwin Hudspiths and their three children, formerly with the Overseas Missionary Fellowship in north Thailand.

In addition to my work at Sangkla, I served on the committee which checked the new translation of the Scriptures into the Sgaw Karen language as spoken in northern Thailand. The translator only had half of Luke left to translate; but the committee was way behind in its work of going over the translation, since we could work only when I could get away from my station. There was some concern that we might not be able to get it all done before I left for furlough (home leave) in August.

On April 15th, 1972, I nearly lost my life in an accident. The annual meeting of the Karen Baptist Convention was held at Musikee village for three days as was a boy scout jamboree for the regional scouts. Dr. John Bissett was helping the scouts, and several American Baptist missionaries attended the Karen Baptist Convention. After the convention, Edy McCarty, one of the American Baptist missionaries, and the youngest children who had attended the convention were flown to Mae Chaem in a police helicopter and the government officials allowed them to stay on the veranda of the local high school from which they could contact the parents to come and get their children. While most of the young people travelled down on rafts in the little mountain stream between the hills, we the missionaries including Dr. John Bissett, hiked two days through the mountains to Mae Chaem, which was where the regional headquarters was located.

While the last group of us were returning in two cars on the last day's journey to Chiang Mai, one moment we were relaxed and thankful that our journey was almost over. The next moment we became aware that the rental car we were in was going faster and faster down the winding mountain road because the brakes had given way and the driver was unable to change gears at that speed. The only way to avoid going over the cliff was to hit the mountain-side – and I got the brunt of the impact.

With a fractured tibia, pelvis, humerus, and 10 ribs, plus a dislocated humerus and clavicle all on the left side, and a fractured ulna and dislocated radius on the right side, I was in pretty bad shock. In fact, I was thought to be dead at first. It was still 5 hours' drive to Chiang Mai where I could get proper treatment at the fine Christian hospital, McCormick Hospital. By

God's grace Dr. Bissett in the same car was not hurt and "just happened" to have both morphine and glucose with him. He administered them at once. I would surely have died on the way if it hadn't been for that. Even so, I was on the critical list for several days, and then suddenly developed difficulty in breathing. A chest surgeon was called in and discovered that my left lung had collapsed and that my right lung had some congestion. He put in a tube to remove air from the pleural cavity, and I got almost immediate relief. In 24 hours, I was like a new person. For almost 2 months I made more rapid progress than folks, including the doctor, thought possible for almost two months. Then a bit of infection in the left tibia set me back a bit. But I was discharged from the hospital on the 19th of July 1972 after three months and three days in the hospital. I convalesced in Maesariang in the home of Dr. Bina Sawyer, one of our ABFMS missionaries who had become a close friend of mine.

Everyone agreed that it was a miracle that I was alive. I am sure that it was because so many people were praying for me even before they knew of the accident, and especially after they did know. Right from the beginning I sensed God's presence with me and had the assurance that God was in control, so I didn't need to worry about anything. And then so many people from all over the world – some of whom I didn't know before – indicated that they were praying for me. Also, so many folks in Chiang Mai went out of their way to cheer me and to help me in every way they could. I was simply overwhelmed. As I thought about it, I realized that this was a taste of the way God intended for us, His children, to care about each other in all of our troubles, no matter what kind they may be. For He planned that we should need each other as well as Himself.

When I thought back over this experience and realized how easily my life could have been snuffed out, I was humbly grateful to God and more desirous than ever that the remainder of my life should be pleasing to Him.

I reached the States on the 20th of September 1972 and was able to see a good orthopedic surgeon on the 2nd of October. He felt that no operations were indicated at that time but ordered physical therapy of various types. Then on November 14th he operated on my right elbow because the two bones of the lower arm had grown together so that I couldn't turn the palm of my hand either up or down. He also stretched the right elbow and the left shoulder while I was unconscious to limber them up and to see how far it was possible to move those joints in various directions.

After three months of treatment my left leg was just about normal, although I still needed to exercise it several times a day in order to keep it from getting stiff. As far as my left shoulder was concerned, the doctor felt that an operation to take care of the deformity would probably not be successful but that I should be able to get nearly full use of it with physical therapy. My elbow was the most difficult joint. The therapist was able to turn my arm so that the palm of the hand turned up and down normally, but she was still unable to stretch my arm out straight or bend it as far as it should go.

Much of my time at home was spent in exercises, but I was happy that I had been allowed to do some deputation in Washington, D.C., and vicinity. Since I was a local girl, a number of requests came for me to speak.

I stayed with a close friend for about six weeks. Then, because it was necessary for her to be hospitalized, I moved to the home of a couple I knew. When they were getting ready to go to Florida for a holiday, I moved on January 19th, 1973, to a home in my hometown.

I received a letter from our home mission worker in Thailand, telling me that four more persons were baptized at Bongti Village during their Christmas celebration that year, and that they had also completed and dedicated a small bamboo chapel. I also received a report that at the end of a week's evangelistic campaign at our school at Sangkla, about half of the 170 pupils indicated that they wanted to accept Christ as their Savior. So, there was cause for praise to God, as well as a need for continued prayer.

I spoke at the Kansas State Women's Conference and at several association meetings in West Virginia. Then after visiting my aunt and uncle in Texas for about a week, I attended the Foreign Missions' Conference and the Furlough Missionaries Conference at Green Lake (Wisconsin) from August 11-21, 1973, visited my sister and her family for several days in Albuquerque, New Mexico, and friends, including retired Burma's missionaries, in southern California.

By God's grace I returned to Thailand, leaving Los Angeles on August 28th, 1973, and arriving in Bangkok on the 31st 1973, with nearly 24 hours each in Tokyo and Hong Kong.

Ever since I got back to the Kwai River Christian Mission (KRCM), it seemed as though one problem after another arose which threatened the work and demanded my time.

There were some real blessings and answers to prayer as well. In the first place, we were without a doctor for nearly 4 years. Then suddenly out of the blue, so to speak, Dr. John Freeman of the Southern Baptist Mission offered himself for 3 years beginning in March 1974, to reopen the hospital and particularly to develop clinics and a public health program in key villages in the district. He came with his wife, Nancy, and 4 vivacious, well-brought-up children, and also added 1 cat, 1 goat, 9 rabbits, 1 baby raccoon, and 1 baby barking deer.

An Australian Baptist nurse, Josie Falla, assigned to the Sangkla Mission, seemed to be a perfect coworker for the doctor, and enjoyed the village work. In 3 villages in particular there was a very good response to the well-baby clinics and family planning program; but when the river became too low for boat travel, the trips were stopped for that and other reasons. Also, it was necessary for Josie to take an early furlough (home leave) due to health reasons. But a new Australian Baptist nurse, Jan Stretton, arrived. The rains were also beginning again, so the village clinics started up again.

In March 1975, our first class of students graduated from the equivalent of junior high school (10th grade). There were only 4 or 5 Christian high schools in the whole country, and entrance for those who had not already been studying in these schools was mainly on the basis of competitive examination. We were very pleased that two of our girls were accepted at one school, and a boy was third on the waiting list for another school. We arranged for some financial aid for these young people. One of the girls was baptized believer and the other girl and the boy were believers but had not yet been able to get their parents' permission to be baptized. (We didn't baptize anyone without their parents' permission until they were able to earn their own living.)

About 7 weeks before school was to reopen the previous year, our school principal suddenly resigned, and the only person with the necessary educational qualifications whom we could find on such short notice was a young and relatively inexperienced fellow who claimed to be a Christian, although later we learned that he had never been baptized. The other

14

teachers on the staff were mostly older and more experienced, but they didn't have as high scholastic qualifications as he did. They were unable to respect him or cooperate with him, so the morale of the school dropped way down with a resulting poor quality of instruction was given. Had we thought that we could find a better person in the middle of the school year, we would probably have dismissed him. But good teachers would not have been likely to leave their jobs before the school year ended, and the law of the country allowed a school to remain open without a qualified principal for a maximum of 3 months only.

But by God's grace, we found a new principal for the following year, who gave promise of having the experience and capability of building up the school scholastically and who was determined that the school would have a strong Christian witness. She was a graduate of Silliman University in the Philippines, and yet was willing to come to this remote area to work at a salary which we could afford to pay. Since most of the teachers would be new that year as well, it seemed that would be easier for her to make the changes she wished. Many of the young people in our school had taken a stand for Christ and seemed to really want to know Him better and live for Him, but so much depended on the spiritual stature of their leaders. We were hopeful that the coming year would be a year of moving forward for the Lord.

Two months before that, ten persons from three villages were baptized in Bambaw Village in the Ratburi District, and the next week we expected to baptize 5 in the Pilokkhi Village and another 5 in Kwitcatoe Village. Also, several were ready for baptism in Bongti Village the previous Christmas, but no ordained minister was free to go there at that time. They decided to wait until the next Christmas when it was expected that not only would there be a few more ready for baptism, but also it was planned at that time to formally establish the Bongti Church as a full-fledged church instead of just a home mission station.

Our work was spread out over a wide geographical area, too wide for one missionary to properly supervise. We were happy that upon their return from furlough (home leave) Rev. Cecil Carder and his wife took the responsibility for the southern part of this work (i.e., the Petchburi and Ratburi Districts and as far north as Bongti Village) in the next month or two. There were many villages in that area where there were persons open to the Christian message, but nobody to instruct them.

Before I returned to the United States in February 1977, a work team, composed of three electricians and one plumber, who at their own or the church's expense went down to Thailand from Australia for about three weeks to help straighten out some of the electrical and plumbing problems on the mission station. (It was impossible to get a plumber or electrician from Bangkok to go up to our station because of the long, tiring trip.) I then had a restful stay in the home of the southeast Asia director of Compassion, Inc., which was helping many of the needy children in our Christian school and hostel with their school and hostel expenses.

On my way to the USA for home leave in August 1977, I spent three happy weeks visiting friends in Australia. The Australian Baptist Missionary Society and the Baptist Union of Sweden worked together with the American Baptist missionaries in Thailand, and so we had formed ourselves into the Thailand Baptist Missionary Fellowship with a common administration. But the Swedes and Aussies sent missionaries and/or funds only for certain aspects of the total mission program of the Thailand Baptist Missionary Fellowship (TBMF). The Australians, for example, particularly with the Lahu tribe of people in northeastern Thailand, and with the TBMF at Sangkla as my co-workers.

While I was in Australia, I visited three former Thailand missionaries, one active missionary from Sangkla who home on home leave was, the parents of Jan Vertigen, and the daughter and son-in-law of the Burmans, who were my co-workers at Sangkla. I also visited the four members of the Australian work team and the families of three of them.

In addition, I also saw quite a bit of the country's beautiful scenery along the eastern side from Newcastle to Melbourne and along the northern and eastern sides of Tasmania Island. I was especially impressed by the thick two-inch long fur on the cattle. (I was told that they grow it in the winter and shed it in the spring, and of course June was wintertime there.) I walked among and fed some kangaroos and a wombat and saw two koala bears in captivity. (They were an endangered species), and saw kookaburras sitting on the tree limbs. I also spoke at several churches and to the monthly meeting of the Victoria State Women's Missionary Society as well as with the board's members. So, you can see, I had an enjoyable time and accomplished quite a bit during my three-week stay.

As for the hospital at Sangkla, after being closed for four years, Dr. John Freeman and his family came and reopened the hospital and trained paramedical personnel to carry on much of the work. He especially emphasized a village health program including Under-Fives' Clinics for the children, antenatal care, and family planning, as well as examination and treatment of the sick – all at a minimal cost. By the beginning of 1978, clinics were held monthly in fourteen villages, besides the community in which the hospital was located. As a result, an improvement of the general health of the villagers in most of those centers and the establishing of friendly contacts made it easier for Christians to go in and witness.

However, when the doctor's term of service was up, we had no resident doctor. Once again, we were able to meet the requirements of the government to keep the hospital open with the nursing staff in charge and a mission doctor from elsewhere coming for a week once every two to three months.

But it meant a great mental and emotional strain on the nurses, also meant that some patients could not be treated at our hospital, and it took a whole day by motorboat, for which the fare was expensive to get to the nearest doctor. In many cases whoever accompanied the patient could not afford to pay hotel bills or even the cost of meals in the town. Furthermore, many of them could only speak their own tribal language and didn't know Thai. This meant they could not communicate with the downriver hospital staff. In real emergencies – like the man who had one side of his face and scalp bitten badly by a tiger and the man a week or two later who was still bleeding from his spleen when he arrived at the hospital ten days after having been kicked in the abdomen. Sometimes a helicopter could be obtained from the border police, and then the trip took only one hour and cost nothing. But at other times, the helicopter was not available or radio service with the authorities downriver could not be established in time.

As for the school, we had real personnel problems for three years in a row. This caused both the scholastic standard and the Christian witness of the institution to deteriorate considerably. But then by God's grace things improved. We phased out the eighth to tenth grades and the government changed the seventh grade over to the junior high department. With only six grades plus a preparatory class to enable the tribal children to learn enough Thai to take the regular course, and with a very fine young man as principal who had many plans for improving all aspects of the school and its program, also had a business manager who was meticulous in filling out all of the forms which the government required and in keeping records and accounts which must be kept.

We were especially excited with the program of village Bible institutes which the Raymond Burmans, a couple from Australia, got underway. They started going to each of the six to seven villages where we spent three to four days in each (as well as the main Sangkla station) three times a year. The first course was an overall Bible survey course and there was a real show of interest on the part of a nucleus of persons in each of the places. In three of the villages some non-Christians attended and showed real interest, too. In most cases I served as interpreter since the Burmans had only learned Thai at that point.

Another cause for encouragement was the formation of the Kwai Noi Association, composed of three churches – the Sangkla Church, the Jordan Church at Kuichatho, and the Pilokkhi Church. Heretofore, the whole work of the Kwai River Christian Mission had been considered a joint mission project of the Church of Christ in Thailand and the Thailand Baptist Missionary Fellowship. The stimulus for the formation of this association had come from several of the national Christian leaders who were anxious that the churches begin to stand on their own feet and begin to take responsibility for the evangelistic outreach themselves (and eventually all of the projects of the Kwai River Christian Mission).

We were very pleased to learn that at the first annual general meeting of the association on March 19-21, 1978, two of our other churches decided to join also and sent representatives. Attendance and interest were good, and it was a joy to see the national Christians doing it all themselves. This was not a mission-initiated or mission-run project. It was their own! The two most important decisions made were (1) to raise the budget for the next year by two-thirds more than the following year, and (2) to take the necessary steps to join the Church of Christ in Thailand as a new district association.

Another bit of news from Sangkla was that Ray and Shirley Burman had taken the school principal and five boys from the hostel with ages between 15 and 22 years old into their own home as an extended family. Their immediate goal was to make room in the over-crowded hostel for new children who otherwise would have no place to stay while going to school and also to try to help the boys develop into useful citizens and hopefully come to know the Lord personally as well. It meant less privacy for the Burmans and for the principal (who would be in charge when the Burmans were on village trips), but they were hoping that the benefits to all concerned would make it worthwhile.

That same year, in order to commemorate 150 years since the first missionary went to work in Thailand, the Protestant Christian churches had been sponsoring a joint-evangelistic program. Seven special crusades, one right after the other, were held in February and March in various cities, and there was a good response in all of them. I took some of our Christians to the one held in Bangkok; and although many people believed that the Thai people wouldn't come to the front to publicly confess Christ, as Westerners are accustomed to do, yet over 100 persons came forward each of the five nights.

In July 15, I was shocked to learn that Shirley Burman had been killed. Her husband, Ray, wrote: "Coming downriver to some special meetings we rounded a bend in the river. Nobody saw the oncoming boat until it was too late. A cry, a bump, and the bow of the other boat came over the side where Shirley was sitting with her back to it. The bow struck her head, and she was knocked unconscious …. She died immediately."

Naturally, that was a great shock to everyone, but the Lord was sustaining Ray and he had peace in his heart concerning the matter. He had already lost two children earlier by accidental deaths, and he was comforted by the assurance that Shirley was now with them and that he would see her and them again. He had one surviving daughter married and living in Australia.

During the between-semester holidays in October Ray took all five boys downriver for a three-day visit in Bangkok (they had never been to a city before) and then three days to a Baptist Youth Conference at our Baptist campgrounds on the gulf. Ray wrote that so far as he knew none of the boys made a commitment to Christ during that time, but that they were impressed to meet so many Thai young people who were Christians and that they would like to return next year. Another one of my co-workers wrote that many folks there in Thailand were seeing Shirley's home going as a challenge for them to take up more responsibility and that the annual station conference was characterized by an unusually loving and caring spirit and evidence of the Spirit's work.

Our hospital had been without a full-time doctor since May 1978. Then, a new doctor, Dr. Phil McDaniel, with his wife and daughter, arrived in Thailand to work at our hospital. But first they had to complete six months of Thai language study, and he also had to take and pass the government medical examination. They visited our station briefly, and my co-workers were favorably impressed with them.

Meanwhile, I had a very profitable ten weeks of study at the Fuller Theological Seminary in Pasadena, California, the School of World Mission. It was still quite fundamental in theology although the other two departments appeared to be more liberal. All of my teachers had worked in Third World countries in mission or church work. Furthermore, about one-third of the students were missionaries on furlough, and another one-third were international students; so, the courses included discussions and illustrations which were quite practical, and I found the courses most stimulating and helpful. I studied Cultural Anthropology, Intercultural Communication, Introduction to the Study of Religion, Training of Leaders in Third World Countries, and Preparation of Programmed Materials. We were encouraged to write out term papers on topics applying what we had been learning to some aspect of the work we were interested in, and I found the research very stimulating and enlightening.

While at the Seminary I attended two walk-through-the-Bible institutes at one of the churches – one in Old Testament and one in New Testament. Many methods were used to help the participants remember the main events of the Bible including their relationship to each other, the geography involved, the books of the Bible telling of each, and practical application to our lives. They were so worthwhile that I decided to go to Indianapolis on April 28 for a Personal Bible Study institute sponsored by the same organization.

On the way back east, I spent two weeks visiting friends and relatives along the way. I enjoyed seeing all whom I visited, but it was especially delightful to meet many of my father's sister's children and some of their families at a family get-together one night. Except for two of the cousins whom I had visited briefly back in 1954, we hadn't seen each other since I was seven years old.

Naturally, I was getting anxious to return to Thailand. From reports, there had been some changes in personnel. By then, the new doctor, Phil McDaniel, and his family had gone up to the station and started working at the hospital. We heard that the government was planning to build a dam about sixty-five kilometers south of us which would result in flooding many of the villages in our area. The Thailand Baptist Missionary Fellowship executive committee appointed a subcommittee to look into the matter.

I left by plane on May 16 from New York City and spent about thirty hours in Frankfurt, Germany, to catch up a bit with the jet lag, then I continued on to Bangkok, arriving May 19 around 12 o'clock noon.

Ray Burman left Thailand to return to Australia before I got back to Thailand, so I missed him. However, he came back again in September 1979 to marry a Chinese Christian and to take her back to his country where they had a pastorate. The five boys who had lived in the Burman home returned to the dorm/hostel before he left. That made the hostel quite crowded.

Phil and Melba McDaniel completed their language study, and Phil passed his Thai medical exam. They had become a real blessing to us all and especially to the medical program. Phil was kept busy enough with patients to know that he was really needed. Melba helped out occasionally at the hospital pharmacy, taught an English class to some of the hospital staff, and took over the station accounts, plus spending time with her three-year-old daughter, Linette, so all that kept her busy.

About ten days after my arrival to Thailand, a church growth seminar on Communicating the Gospel and Evangelizing the Buddhists was held at the Southern Baptists' lovely conference grounds at Pattaya on the Gulf of Thailand. I and two of my home mission workers attended. There were about sixty people in all, and the institute was a real blessing. The guest speaker was Rev. Lakshonan Peiris, an Anglican clergyman/evangelist from Sri Lanka who had been having an effective ministry among the Buddhists in his country for about seven years. He gave us many helpful insights and illustrations to help us see how to present the Christian truths in a way that the Buddhists could understand and so be attracted to Christ. How grateful I was to our loving Father for timing this conference near the beginning of this term of service as I was trying to seek the Lord's guidance as to how to reach the Buddhists around us more effectively.

In October, a couple in their late forties were baptized. They had turned to the Lord in desperation because people in the village were frequently bothered by evil spirits who claimed to be the wife's spirit. So, the people who were being bound by fear of the spirits, threatened to kill her if she didn't take steps so that such demonic activity would cease. She tried every remedy the Buddhist priests and the leaders in their occult practices knew how to administer, but the trouble persisted. Then one of our workers told them that Jesus had power over all evil spirits. They then turned to Jesus and found that, true to his Word, he had delivered them and there was no more trouble after their baptism. Praise the Lord!

In November, our hostel father Olivepa had to go to Bangkok for major surgery. This was followed by complications which had to be expected at his age (85yrs). Because of this his daughter Olivia (our public health nurse) had to go to Bangkok for a couple of months to nurse him. Then in January his wife Olivemo decided to go down with Loes de Vos, one of my co-workers in Thailand, to visit him and on the way, they were involved in a very serious accident ... Loes suffered concussion, chipped a piece of bone off the vertebrae in her neck and had many cuts and bruises and it was two months before she was well enough to make the journey back to Sangkla. Olivemo, we think, was killed instantly. It was hard to explain what Olivemo's death meant to Sangkla. She had been hostel-mother since the early sixties when the hostel was started. She was a strong wise person always there when needed. She served on our mission committee, was the friend and confident of many of the local people and mother to countless hostel children; in fact, a very real mother to many of the children who had no mother or were only able to travel home once a year. Seeing these children, some only five or six years old, gathered in a lot larger group at her funeral with big bunches of wildflowers they had collected as their last tribute to her, and lost or confused looks on their faces, I realized something of their loss. And of course, to her own family the loss was even greater. Sangkla Mission lost two great women of God in the last two years, and we were very conscious of our loss.

There were also some good things happening:

(1)   we had finished the first six-month term of our nurse aide training program and could see some improvement in the work and understanding of some who were new recruits.

(2)   The Lord provided us with a couple to take over the work of the hostel. They came with very good recommendations.

(3)   We had a good year at school and gave thanks to God for the headmaster and teachers we had.

Also, the eight boys who made decisions in October seemed to be going on well and most had been baptized. I made an appeal in one of my talks in church and the son of one of our evangelists made a public confession of his faith. It was so good to see these young people growing in the Christian faith. One big disappointment for us was DeWood the nurse- aide; she seemed to have lost her interest in the things of God. For people like DeWood who lived away from the mission compound Christian life was difficult. In her village there was absolutely no evidence of anything Christian, life revolved around the temple and spirit worship. Then, too, our church at Sangkla was basically Karen and DeWood was a Thai speaking Mon so that when she returned to Sangkla it was difficult for her to have fellowship with people who were culturally different.

On December 23, 1979, the Thanongsri Church was officially established as a church under the Church of Christ in Thailand (CCT), and in March 1980, it officially joined the Kwai River Christian Mission (KRCM) at its annual meeting. At this same meeting, the Association appointed Thra Lawwaddee as a part-time traveling home mission worker to visit and strengthen the churches and to witness to non-Christian villagers as he had opportunity.

In September at the annual station conference of the Kwai River Christian Mission, Thra Lawwaddee and Thra Bo Boe, the pastor of the Sangkla Church, were ordained. It was the first time that there had been an ordained minister resident in any of the five districts in which the Kwai River Christian Mission worked. Up to that time, when anyone wanted to be baptized, arrangements had to be made for someone to come from another part of Thailand or from Burma in order to perform the ceremony.

Following the ordination service five persons were baptized: a Thai school teacher, one Mon and one Karen clinic worker, and two students. The Mon man was the first from his community and only the third Mon in the whole district to accept Christ. The Thai teacher also came from a Buddhist background. One of the students was a girl whose family told her frankly that if she were baptized, they would be compelled to disown her lest the spirits be offended. Fortunately, one of our Christian families whose daughter was a close friend of hers invited her to be in their family when school was not in session.

There seemed to be a real stirring of the Spirit in the southernmost district in which we have a home mission worker. Six members of the Suan Phoeng Church at Banbaw Village have begun really to concentrate on praying for and visiting daily specific non-Christians, and to seek to become real friends with them and to witness as they had opportunity to do so naturally. In addition to the regular midday worship service held in one of the Christian homes, they met Sunday mornings about 7:00 a.m. at the home of one or another interested non-Christians for singing, prayer, and discussion of some Bible passages. Quite a few non-Christians came also to listen. A group of them went about once a month to Huay Phak Village, and six persons had been baptized that year, including a man over 60 years of age. The worker, Nai Charoen, and his youngest brother, Choat, travelled frequently to nearby villages on a motorcycle, which was a present from a Korean church, to visit the villagers in a friendly fashion and to witness as they had opportunity. They also visited the Christians in Anata Village at least once a month.

The Khao Laem Dam was being built in connection with a new hydro-electric project and would result in flooding the location of twenty-five villages, the Sangkla district headquarters area, plus the premises of the Kwai River Christian Mission. Everyone had to move. However, relocation moved frustratingly slowly. By August 1983, the district headquarters had nearly completed its various public buildings and quarters for its personnel. However, the villagers still didn't know to which plot of land they were to be reassigned, so they couldn't do anything in connection with moving. They would be given assignments towards the end of the rainy season so that they could rebuild and prepare new rice fields and move before the beginning of the following rainy season (May 1984), which was the time scheduled for closing the dam.

The Kwai River Christian Mission at first planned to move to a nice piece of land near the new district headquarters. But then we learned that the government had decided to build a hospital of its own; the question arose as to whether we were warranted in building a new hospital there. So, a wait-and-see-how-things-develop attitude was taken. Because of the uncertainty of the continuance of the medical program, the school and boarding department decided that rather than be in the same area with the big government school, they would rather move to the northwest relocation area where most of the Karens would be relocated in order to minister among those who would otherwise have opportunity for only a very low level of education. However, since our school only went through sixth grade, whereas the government had facilities to teach through ninth, we also wanted to have a hostel in the district headquarters area—probably coupled with a Christian center program.

One of my American Baptist co-workers, Ben Dickerson's wife, Doris, took over the evangelism department of the Kwai River Christian Mission.

Most of our home mission efforts had been among Pwo and Sgaw Karens, but we had one Mon working among the Mon people for about ten years. In all that time only one couple accepted Christ. But then all of a sudden five families decided to accept the Lord. When that worker decided to move to a new area several additional families decided that they also wanted to take a stand for Christ—this in spite of some persecution of the first group! The worker agreed to stay on until the end of May to instruct these new converts. He would also try to find a new worker to come and work among these people. We started weekly Bible classes there on Sundays using Burmese, which some of the Mon understood.

Meanwhile, I was busy most of September and October in 1984, speaking in churches-first in Ohio, then North Dakota, New Hampshire, the Scranton area of Pennsylvania, Connecticut, Maine, and New Jersey, in that order. I had two six-day and two three-day periods free during that time, so I used some of that time to visit friends and relatives more or less along the way. I enjoyed visiting with those whom I had known before, as well as meeting new friends and telling about the work and life in Thailand. There was only one problem-too much good food! Although

I tried to be careful, I still gained four pounds during the two months, whereas, the Associated Mission Medical Office had advised me to lose twenty pounds.

On the night of September 8th, Dr. Lois Visscher, the lady missionary doctor who had been helping at our hospital for over a year, was viciously beaten and stabbed in an attempted murder in her home. It followed the death of a seriously ill or wounded outpatient and was evidently done in revenge because she didn't stop in the middle of an operation on another patient and come out to treat that one. (The nurse had done what she could.) After reading her own X-rays she was sure that medically she had no hope of recovery, so she gave full instructions concerning the disposal of her remains and property. However, the Christian community prayed earnestly, and by God's grace she didn't die. The next day she was flown downriver by a border police helicopter and was admitted to the Bangkok Christian Hospital, where she was operated upon twice. (Her lung, diaphragm, and liver had received stab wounds.) After about three weeks when the fever and infection failed to respond to treatment, she was flown to California. Finally, it was discovered that she had a chronic amebic infection. She was not aware that it had flared up in her wounded liver, and, of course, ameba is not affected by antibiotics. Once the right treatment was given, she recovered.

In November and the first few days of December I had a fair number of speaking engagements in churches connected with the District of Columbia Convention, most of its churches were dually aligned. This was not very tiring since I could live and sleep at my home base.

On December 9th I had a cataract removed from my left eye at the Wills Eye Hospital in Philadelphia and an intraocular lens implanted. I had no problems and hardly any handicap post-operatively. Fortunately, the vision in my left eye was good enough that I could read and write all right even though the right eye didn't focus together with it. I found that I depended mostly on my "new" eye for distance and my "old" eye for reading and writing.

As for the Mon worker, he had been unable to find a new worker to replace himself, so he stayed on to work with the new converts even though his wife and children had already gone back to be with his mother-in-law.

During my home leave, I had the opportunity to share something of the work of the Kwai River Christian Mission (KRCM)with which I had been connected. I attended three seminars which helped me in my work as well as three prayer conferences. The last one was the Baptist Prayer Conference in which nine different Baptist denominational groups cooperated.

I had the opportunity to visit some friends and all the relatives in the course of my deputation travels. Then beginning March 30th, I used one of thirty-day bus passes offered in those days and traveled from Washington, D.C. to Virginia and to a number of places in Florida, then across the southern part of the country and on to southern California, up the West Coast as far as Seattle, and back by the northern route as far as St. Paul, Minnesota. The main purpose of the trip was to visit friends and relatives, and I succeeded in visiting fifty-five households as well as speaking in four churches. The folks visited included twenty former missionary colleagues, two Christians whom I had met in Thailand where they were working, two of my nurses' training classmates, three of my seminary classmates, four relatives, and sixteen families who had migrated from Burma. Eight of those visited I hadn't seen for thirty or more years and another six for seventeen to twenty-nine years. One was a cousin whom I didn't even know existed until a few months before the trip. So, you can see that the trip meant a lot of happy reunions and catching up on past experiences, and it meant a great deal to me. I also visited two missionary families on furlough in Sweden and a cousin and his wife in Austria on my return trip to Thailand.

My assignment for this term of service was to work full time with the churches which had grown out of the work of the Kwai River Christian Mission (KRCM) in order to help them become strong, evangelistic, and self-supporting churches– no small task! It had been decided that I should live in the town of Kanburi (Kanchanaburi), since it was more centrally located, as far as the churches were concerned, from there traveled out to the villages. It was a new experience for me, as I had always lived in a village situation up till that time. The Lord's will for me. He provided a house, unexpected contacts to help me with purchases and arrangements, and a girl who lived nearby to help me with the housework. The girl who came to help me with the housework accepted the Lord as her Savior and Lord and was baptized at the end of November. It was a joy to see her grow in her knowledge of the Word and her desire to share the Good News with others.

I learned that Sangkla where the Kwai River Christian Mission (KRCM) compound was located, everything was in a state of chaos. The buildings were being torn down and rebuilt in the new locations while the missionaries and other workers still had to live somewhere, and some hospital work had to be carried on. But everyone was willing to live and work under temporarily inconvenient circumstances for the sake of the work. Residences were built for the Bennett Dickersons and the workers. At the northwestern relocation area none of the buildings were really finished, but the doctor's residence, six teachers' houses, and five workers' quarters were enough finished that they could be lived in. The school and hospital took several weeks to finish, and the hostel for elementary students were being completed. While a number of the hostel students lived at the principal's house, since he had bought a piece of property across the road from the new mission premises. The rest of the hostel children were taken in by other teachers. In the meantime, the government permitted the school to open ten days late (i.e., June 1st).

I also learned that about the end of April, the hospital patients were moved from the wards and crowded into the central rotunda and a little food shop building at the back. Then the roofing tiles, doors, and windows from the wards were used in the new building. The hospital officially closed as of June 1st and opened at the new location on June 18th. However, several in-patients could not be discharged yet—the one whose leg was in traction and a severe burn case, among others. Also a few outpatients still came each day. Two or three truckloads of hospital furniture, equipment, and/or supplies were transferred nearly every day to the new location about twelve miles away. However, only after the hospital was officially closed could the remainder of the roof, windows, and doors be removed and used in the new building.

Our mission was grateful that the Australian Baptists sent several work teams to do all the electrical and plumbing installation in the relocated buildings.

God sent hostel parents for the new junior high hostel, Rev. Wut Boonlert and his wife. Both of them had had the experience of living in a number of hostels as students and were both fairly highly educated from the Thai point of view. They began making improvements in the hostel discipline, program, etc. Wut had an interest in agriculture and cut down on expenses by having the hostel students help raise pigs, poultry, and vegetables. He was working with the local group of Christians who met for worship every Sunday at the hostel. He also made a point of becoming friends with and witnessed informally to the local non-Christians in the community.

Starting in May of 1980 a big tourist promotion feature was the "Bridge over the River Kwai Week" festival. The various government departments and a few private businesses displayed exhibits of their work and accomplishments. They also sold products connected with their department or business. In 1985 the festival was held November 28 through December 4, and the local Christians invited us to join with them in setting up a Christian exhibit. In addition to Bibles in various languages, Christian literature for sale, large wall pictures showing scenes from the life of Christ, and the gospel message on wall charts. Video tapes were shown of the Life of Christ according to Luke, the Ten Commandments, Solomon and the Queen of Sheba, and a film showing the bold witness of Christians in the days of the Roman emperors' persecutions. Also, a total of about 50,000 tracts, Scripture selections, and Christian literature were distributed free as well as about 100 application blanks for a Bible correspondence course. An average of about 100 people a day looked in on some part of the exhibit.

After my return to Thailand, I visited all but one of the Christian groups which met regularly for worship in the area of the Kwai River Christian Mission's work, most of them several times.

[See map to picture their location]

In April 1985, there were now thirteen communities where groups of Christians met regularly for worship:

(1) As for <u>The Sangkla Christian Church</u>, which had moved from the old location to the northwestern relocation area called Huay Malai; the congregation was composed of Thais, Pwo Karens, Sgaw Karens, Mons, Americans, and Australians.

(2) There were six Mon Christian families at Namkert whose membership was in the Sangkla Christian Church. One family accepted Christ about four years before that, the rest about two years later. We printed a little illustrated booklet. It presented Christ in terms which the non-Christian Mon could understand and respond to.

(3) A group of Christians was meeting at the junior high hostel at the northern relocation area called Sangkla. They organized as a church that year.

(4)   The Jordan Church met in the home of a different member each week until they had put up a church building.

(5)   Kuichatho was the village where the Jordan Church was originally located. Some of the members moved just above the expected level of the new reservoir but some of the non-Christians were still at the old site. The water level did not reach its peak the previous year we were there. The non-Christians were saying that they no longer had any Buddhist monks or monastery, so perhaps it would be better to become Christians. That's why some of the Christians were staying nearby.

(6)   The Pilokkhi Christians, who were mostly Sgaw Karen refugees from Burma, were organized as a church, but a home mission worker was leading them until they could find a pastor. They relocated to a new site not far from the edge of the reservoir. The church was considered a branch of the Sangkla Christian Church. They had built a temporary bamboo chapel, since only by the end of the rainy season in October, would they have known for sure how extensive the reservoir would be.

(7)   A group of Burma refugees living at Songkalia began meeting weekly for worship.

(8)   The Tanaosri Church at Bongti Village was our strongest church and most enthusiastic group of Christians, but as the result of personality conflicts and the pull of the things of the world they had become the weakest church. One of the most influential members was made not only headman of that village but also later made the head (called karnnan) of three villages, including his own. All his civil responsibilities, as he tried to improve conditions and settle disputes, absorbed all his time so that he rarely got to church. Many other members followed his example.

(9)   The Suanphoeng Church at Huay Namnak was composed mainly of Sgaw Karen refugees from Burma and continued to be quite active.

The following groups of Christians were mostly Thai-born Pwo Karens whose membership was in the Suanphoeng Church but met for worship in their own communities:

- Christians at Banbaw.
- Christians at Hua Klum.
- Christians at Huay Phak.

(10) The Pa Deng group was a group of fairly new Christians, the first ones besides the worker and his wife having been baptized just two years previously. They were enthusiastic and their love and harmony in working together was a testimony to the non-Christians around them, including the government officials.

All the above church groups were organized together as the Gethsemane Association. It was the association to which I had been assigned.

The big event was the 25th Anniversary Celebration of the Kwai River Christian Mission (KRCM) held October 11-13, 1985, just prior to the annual station conference. The Thai Christian drama group called Ligay came and performed the first two nights of the celebration as well as the first night of the station conference. Their performances were of high quality with beautiful costumes and scenery–the type of drama which the Thai appreciate but with a message from the Bible brought out in the end. A number of guests including representatives from the Church of Christ in Thailand (CCT), the Thailand Baptist Missionary Fellowship (TBMF), the Thailand Karen Baptist Convention, the Thailand Lahu Baptist Convention, and the 12th District Association of the CCT (our Chinese Baptists) came for the celebrations.

As the relocated buildings on our premises had been completed except for a few minor details, the hospital, the school, and the two hostels for elementary school children (i.e., boys' and girls' dorms) were officially dedicated by a ceremony in which their new signboards were unveiled. On Sunday, the Sangkla Christian Church also had a brief dedication of its relocated church building. The history of the KRCM since its beginning was reviewed and five national Christians who had been working with the KRCM for more than fifteen years were given special recognition. The one with the longest years of service was Mr. Tha Din (better known to us as Olivepa) who had worked with us for twenty-four of the twenty-five years of the work. He was in his eighties by that time, and he was still serving as translator of the letters from students receiving support from Compassion, Inc. The second one, Thramu Sai Kham, had been one of our home mission workers for twenty-three years. Thirteen persons were baptized Sunday morning nine here from the Sangkla Church and four from the Jordan Church.

We had a peculiar situation there—the local villagers in the area where the KRCM worked were slow to accept the Gospel and we went ahead to develop medical and educational work in the hope that as we helped alleviate the people's needs in those ways, it would help prepare their hearts for the Gospel message. The result was that the hospital, school, and hostel departments of the work were well developed before there was even one church. Later, when there were three churches, they decided to organize into an association which they called the Gethsemane Association. As other churches were formed, they also joined it. However, this association was not directly related to the KRCM or to any other group. They wanted to become a district association of the Church of Christ in Thailand. They did not want to join another district association because of the language problem—most associations used Thai, whereas many of the Karens were not at home in that language. All members of the churches were automatically members of both the KRCM and the Gethsemane Association, and each of these two organizations had an evangelism committee. Naturally, there was overlapping and no clear-cut division of responsibilities between the two groups. So, at the station conference a vote was taken to ask the evangelism committee of the two organizations to work together during the following year to seek to coordinate the work and lay the groundwork for turning all of the work of the KRCM evangelism department over to the association.

In addition to the evangelistic work of the KRCM and of the association, several of the churches had set up their own evangelism projects.

(1) The Jordan Church had called a team of Pwo Karen Bible School graduates from Don Yaung Village to lead a program of "preparing the soil" of the hearts of non-Christian Pwo Karens in the area for the Gospel by use of their traditional songs and dances to convey the Christian message.

The older people showed interest, although it didn't seem to appeal to the younger generation, which had become more Thai-ized.

(2) An evangelistic project had been set up at Huay Klum Village connected with the Suan Phoeng Church as a result of the concern of the worker at Pa Deng Village six-hours-journey away for the nurture of the Christians at Huay Klum who had been without leadership. A piece of land approximately two-thirds of an acre in size had been donated, a bamboo and thatch house large enough to use for meetings as well as for cooking and sleeping was constructed, and the worker was spending a week each month there to teach and encourage the believers and to fellowship with and witness to the non-believers. An evangelistic matching fund, using special gifts from overseas, had enabled financial help to be given to match the donations of the villagers and other interested national Christians. Because the villagers were quite poor, their donations of labor and supplying of building materials had been considered at the equivalent monetary value had the materials been bought or labor hired. This project was started in June, and there was quite a spirit of interest and enthusiasm among the villagers. In fact, the Christians at the nearby village of Huay Phak begged the worker to worship with them also on the Sunday that he was at Huay Klum. On September 1st, ten new Christians (five from each of the two villages) were baptized. As the work grew, the worker turned the work over to a full-time Christian worker in each village.

As for myself, I was away from home more than I was at home - averaged thirteen days a month at home during the period of January through October 1985, I was at home most of November. Being on the KRCM Executive Committee meant at least one trip a month to Sangkla. I also visited the villages where we had Christians worshipping regularly to teach, encourage, and discuss problems and plans. I was happy to do this, but at the same time it was somewhat tiring to live out of a backpack and to travel for a number of hours at a time. I was also glad that the Christians, both national and missionary, were making use of my house as a rest stop during their travels. It saved them hotel expenses and they could relax in a homier atmosphere. It also kept me in touch with what was going on in the various villages. I felt that this was a real ministry and one of the reasons the Lord arranged for me to rent a house in the town instead of living in a Karen village as in the previous years. Often folks who came brought some fresh fruit or vegetables, dried or smoked meat or fish, bought a gift of food from the market, and I also grew some vegetables and fruit. Papaya and jackfruit trees were already in the yard when I moved, and they produced a large number of big fruits. So, I was happy to feed those who cared to eat there. When I was able to be at home for a few days at a stretch, I worked in the garden, which was a relaxing change from what I had been doing.

My home was then the KRCM guest house which was more central to our work than my former location at Sangkla. It meant that much of the time there were guests at my house, persons passing through the town on their way to somewhere else, or persons who had come to town on business, or patients needing to get more specialized medical treatment than they could get locally. I praise the Lord for sending a Karen woman, Grace Sein, to be my companion and to be hostess/house manager for me; because I, myself, wasn't home very much of the time. There had been frequent trips to the villages where we had Christian work, meetings at Sangkla, Bangkok, and Chiangmai, business trips to Bangkok, and trips taking patients to various hospitals. It had often been tiring yet rewarding when it resulted in helping others in need.

As I looked back over my time that term in Thailand, I sensed that God placed me there with the KRCM to be His agent during this phase of the work. My thoughts went back to 1973, when Robert (Bob) Johnson, the area representative for Thailand, sent for me to go and see him at Valley Forge. He informed me that they were thinking of closing down the Kwai River Christian Mission (KRCM) because so much money had been invested in the project, yet there had been such meager results. I begged him to wait a little longer, because the first three local persons (all young people) had accepted Christ shortly before that, and I felt that they were only the first fruits. Sixteen years later, the work had spread into seven other districts in over four provinces. The six churches, one branch church, plus the fourteen preaching stations with a combined membership of more than 500 baptized believers had been organized into an association and had just recently been accepted into the Church of Christ in Thailand (CCT) as their 16th District Association. A separate organization with practically the same constituency had agreed to become fully integrated. At the association's annual meeting, April 17-23 the KRCM became fully integrated with the 16th District Association. So, one phase of the work was coming to a close, and a new phase, under Thai leadership was about to begin. I praise the Lord for allowing me to be there up throughout that time.

That work was originally a joint project of the Church of Christ (Disciples) and the American Baptists. One of its primary goals was to reach the members of the Telakhon sect, a messianic religious group composed mainly of Pwo and Sgaw Karens, which stressed pure moral behavior, strict adherence to the Karen language and culture, taboos forbidding the eating of domesticated meat, and participation in various rites and ceremonies. They believed that if they observed these things faithfully, they would eventually have their own kingdom and rule over the peoples around them. Included in their traditions was the prophecy concerning the "lost book." This "lost book" was their Guidebook. It told them how to live and contained life's answers. The book was lost during the 13th century when they traveled south from China. The tradition also said that one day a younger white brother would restore it to them.

However, although a century earlier, larger numbers of Karens in Burma responded to the coming of the white missionaries and the Bible they translated and printed in Karen as being a fulfilment of the above prophecy, the Telakhon turned out to be resistant. Like the Jews of Jesus' day, they were looking for an earthly kingdom, and material and political assistance from the white man. So, four expeditions in the early 1960s failed to find any bridge which could be used to help these people–medically, educationally, or spiritually. Having heard via the grapevine that there was by then a more open attitude, we made another expedition. It was true that many of them were responsive and wanted us to teach and guide them, but the leaders were still afraid to allow us to work with the people. Then, just a month before that (in March) two of our Karen workers went for another visit and found the people eager for us to visit them regularly. Even the "poojite" (the top leader) gave permission for us to come and teach–if we didn't talk against their religion. Some of the leaders said that when the present "poojite" died (and he was already quite old), the Telakhon religion would come to an end. So, if we were there, ready to step in and guide them to the Lord, there was hope that before long, the whole sect would turn to Christ. The presentation of a project for reaching the Telakhon for Christ was planned for the annual meeting.

The Kwai River Christian Mission, at its annual meeting in April 1989, voted to integrate with the local Gethsemane Baptist Association, and on the 23rd of that month, the association was formally welcomed into the Church of Christ in Thailand as its 16th District Association. That gave security and status to the association, which was much desired, because in the past, when the Karens began to evangelize in non-Christian villages, government officials would ask them with what organization they were connected. To say that they were connected with the Kwai River Christian Mission (KRCM) did not make a good impression on the officials because it smacked of propaganda to introduce a foreign religion. But they could reply that they were connected with the CCT, which was one of the four Protestant organizations recognized by the Thai government. They were secure. Furthermore, they took the opportunity to consult with CCT officials, attended training institutes, and received visits and encouragement from CCT leaders. Those officers helped the new association to grow spiritually and otherwise.

I left Thailand on July 21st as planned and spent about 14 days with Gam and Alice Shae at the Sabah Theological Seminary at Kota Kinabalu, Malaysia. I spent part of the first day catching up on some much-needed sleep but had a chance to visit with fellow Christians at both the noon and the evening meals. On the next day, which was Sunday, I visited several small churches, after which the Shaes took me up into the mountains for a picnic lunch. I spent the next night at a hotel in Kuala Lumpur and then left for Los Angeles, where I visited retired American Baptist missionaries, Louise Giffin and Allison Osborne. Bob Johnson and his wife, recently retired from International Ministries, ABC/USA, took us all out to dinner at a Chinese restaurant. We then returned to Louise's apartment for refreshments and fellowship with other residents of the Pilgrim Place—mostly former missionaries. From there I went to Green Lake, WI for the Conference for Overseas Missionaries on home assignment followed by the World Missions Conference. Highlights of the World Missions Conference for me were a challenging message by Dr. John Sundquist, the new executive director of International Ministries, thought-provoking Bible studies led by Dr. Manfred T. Brauch, acting dean and acting president of Eastern Baptist Theological Seminary, and the most moving commissioning service I have ever attended.

The rest of August and the first twelve days of September were spent relaxing, visiting friends, and catching up on reports and correspondence. Then followed a period of deputation through the first Sunday of December. I spoke in the Cleveland, Philadelphia, and Providence associations and in the Washington D.C. Convention's World Missions Conference as well as in Indiana. I also visited friends enroute to these places.

I decided to retire on April 1st the following year (1990), finishing deputation in Michigan on that day, which was a Sunday, to return to Maryland the next day where I remained until April 15th. Then I spent about two months travelling around the country in order to visit friends and relatives and also spoke at a few churches along the way.

I was very pleased and grateful to the Lord that I had the opportunity to return to Thailand for one more year–that time as a volunteer. The Thailand Baptist Missionary Fellowship had asked me to prepare language study materials for the missionaries who needed to learn the Sgaw Karen language. I went out to the villages in various areas of north Thailand in order to record sermons, prayers, stories, conversations, etc., to serve as the basis for the lessons. I also wanted to become better acquainted with the work of the Thailand Karen Baptist Convention. So, I returned to Thailand at the end of June, and I stayed with Dr. Bina Sawyer.

I had received a few letters from Thailand and want to share the following bits of news with you:

News from Thailand was encouraging:

(1) Christmas celebrations were held in six villages in Ratburi and Prachaub provinces, although we only have two churches in the area. There were baptismal services in three of them with a total of eleven new church members. Each candidate gave a brief testimony before being baptized.

(2) The Christian Center program in Kanburi Town was getting underway. Compassion, International was finding sponsors for the 190 registered children from the slums in the program. Most of their school expenses, including books, school uniforms, and a nourishing noon meal would be provided by the sponsors' monthly contributions. The children would be divided into

groups, each of which was to go to the Christian Center every week at a scheduled time on Saturday or Sunday for Christian education. The director, Wut Boonlert, was a seminary graduate.

(3) The association officers soon found that administering the work formerly done by the Kwai River Christian Mission was quite a time-consuming job, especially when none of the four officers were very experienced in accounting. Soon they voted to hire a full-time office worker beginning April 1st when the school year ended. It turned out that the present girls' hostel mother had studied bookkeeping and typing, so she took the job. It was easier to find a new hostel mother than to find an office worker willing to work "out in the sticks."

(4) The chairman of the association wrote that the big need now is for discipleship training. They know how to win people to Christ but need help in nurturing and training the new converts so that they become strong witnesses for Christ.

I arrived in Bangkok the morning of the 28th of August having flown by way of London. Between taking care of various matters and having a short visit with friends with whom I had worked in the past in Kanburi and in Huay Malai in Sangkla District. It involved an overnight 10-houir bus trip from Kanburi to Chiangmai, then a 4-hour trip the next afternoon to Maesariang – my new home.

I stayed at the home of Dr. Bina Sawyer, a single woman BIM missionary doctor who formerly worked in Burma as I did. She was taking a holiday in Maine when I arrived, and she got back home only a week after. However, I had stayed with her quite a few times before, and her servants took good care of me; so, I had no problems.

A nurse named Amporn whose brain was damaged when she was struck down by a car in Bangkok resulting in partial paralysis of the left arm and leg, lived downstairs in Bina's house with her mother. She was able to walk slowly using a four-pronged cane but didn't use her left arm. The hospital was just across the street, and she worked there sitting down. She told new patients where to register, gave out medicines prepared by the pharmacy, and instructing the patients how to take them. Since many patients had little or no education, it was important to make sure they understood the doctor's orders. In the late afternoon Monday – Wednesday Amporn had a children's PTL club where she taught children who came to her home Christian songs and choruses, Bible verses, and a bit of English conversation. She always kept cheerful, and her life was quite a testimony to everyone.

Bina and I lived upstairs except that the kitchen, used by both us and Amporn's mother, was downstairs. We ate our meals on a table on the back veranda overlooking about a half-mile stretch of paddy fields with 'tree-covered mountains beyond. Because this was the latter part of the rainy season, everything was lovely and green. We usually got a nice breeze on the veranda also, so I often sat at the table there to do my writing, reading, etc., in the mornings.

Besides Bina and I there were 4 missionary couples and 3 other single women missionaries living there in Maesariang who got together Sunday evenings for a prayer meeting with refreshments and fellowship afterwards. Two of the couples came out under the new Tribes Mission and 1 single woman was under the Overseas Missionary Fellowship (OMF): The missionaries under the Thailand Baptist Missionary Fellowship (TBMF) to which the BIM missionaries belonged were Duane and Marcia Binkley and Kim Brown from BIM plus Dr. Tom and Betty Roberts who were special service workers at the hospital. The other single woman missionary was' from the Baptist: Missionary Society in England, which was also a part of TBMF, and was named Jacqui Wells. She was already studying Sgaw Karen using the old book which I had prepared back in 1957.

Everyone who used the language book said that there were too many new words and too few drills in each lesson so that the vocabulary and sentence structure didn't get mastered, so I needed to work on that.

The preparation of the new language book has moved along slowly, partly because of the time-consuming job of preparing supplementary lesson material for Jacqui Wells.

The second reason was that I have had no training in the preparation of language books, read all the materials on methods of language learning I could find. I also examined sample materials in Thai, Akha, and Pwo Karen. At the end of January, two persons began using the lessons, enabling me to get feedback from both of them as well as their teachers. Later on, I checked the materials in other areas of northern Thailand to make sure that I had used vocabulary, which was understood there, and to take note of any colloquial differences in pronunciation which should be indicated in footnotes.

I wasn't just busy doing language lessons all day every day, however. A few of the more important events I participated in were as follows:

1) August 23 – 26 (1991) I helped escort a tour group from the Calvary Baptist Church in Washington D.C. around Chiang Rai and Chiang Mai in northern Thailand to see some of the Christian work (some of which I had not seen myself before.)

2) On the afternoon of November 3rd, I attended the 25th anniversary of the Mae Sariang Christian Hospital held in the outpatients' waiting room.

3) On November 22nd all of the Baptist, New Tribes, and Overseas Missionary Fellowship missionaries and their families who were in the Mae Sariang area (a total of 25 adults and 9 children) had Thanksgiving dinner together. This was followed by a brief worship service which included an explanation of the origin of the holiday for the benefit of the non-Baptist missionaries. There were also games before supper for the children and videos afterward enjoyed by all.

4) The highlight of the year was my trip to Burma December 13 — 20, where I saw many former friends and acquaintances, including five of my former protégés. December 14 – 16 commemorated the 175th anniversary of Adoniram Judson's arrival in Burma and the 125th anniversary of the Myanmar (Burma) Baptist Convention. A total of 15,000 guests from all over Burma were fed two meals a day, and a record of 20,000 attended the main Sunday morning service. The tribal costumes were colorful, the displays in the booths of the ethnic and area conventions which made up the MBC were interesting and informative, the flower arrangements at the front of the memorial hall were beautiful, the pageant of Judson's life was well done and very moving, and everything was well organized and carried out smoothly. The theme was "Service and Sacrifice" with the cross in a crown as the symbol.

5) I joined in Christmas celebrations with the other missionaries as well as with the Karen Baptist Church there in Mae Sariang during Christmas week.

6) January 8 – 13, I taught "The Life of Christ" at a women's training institute at Tho-pa-Kha Village, about an hour's trip by car from Mae Sariang Town. About 70 women attended.

American Baptist missionary, Ben Dickerson, and Allan Eubank (a Presbyterian missionary) together with the Karen Evangelist named David spent two weeks of November with the Telakhon. They taught Christian beliefs and learned more of the Telakhon beliefs and the meanings behind their rituals and symbolism in an effort to discover which ones they could continue to use if they became Christians. The Telakhon had not yet agreed to accept Christ but only accept teaching from the Christians. The government tried to step up its attempts to get the Telakhon to send their children to a government school and to become Buddhists. The Telakhon resisted any group that did not have a high moral code. Most Telakhon were also illiterate and didn't understand the ways of the government. That was why they wanted a missionary to come and live with them full time. (The Karen Christian couple living among them only had a junior high education.)

I was given permission to remain in Thailand for another year in order to continue the preparation of language study materials. I had informed Pilgrim Place, the retirement community in Claremont, California, to which I planned to move that I would be ready to enter at the end of July 1992, or as soon thereafter as there was a vacancy.

Although I remained in Maesariang during my time in Thailand, the headquarters of the Thailand Baptist Missionary Fellowship (TBMF) to which Board of International Ministries (BIM) belonged moved in June 1991 from Bangkok to Chiangmai, which was the hub of north Thailand. The main reason was that Bangkok had been expanding so greatly that rents became exorbitant.

As I was thinking back over my 18 years of service in Burma, that which gave me the greatest sense of fulfilment was the fact that of the 7 girls who stayed with me at one time or another during their late teens and early twenties, 6 of them went into full-time Christian work, one of these named Diana became the executive secretary of the Pwo Karen Women's Federation and as such she visited and held training institutes twice a year in each of the 6 associations, teaching women' s work, youth work, and Christian Home. She was chosen as one of the 3 delegates from the Burma Baptist Convention to the World Council of Churches assembly, which was held in Australia in February. I saw her in Bangkok for 2 days before she left for the meetings. She spent a week with me in Thailand afterwards. What a joy to see how the Lord was using her!

April 2-5, I attended the annual meeting of the Thailand Karen Baptist Convention (TKBC) held in a village several hours' trip north of Chiangmai. About 1000 attended. The reports showed that as of March 31, 1991, the Convention had 67 full-fledged churches and 226 branch churches with a total membership of 11,983 organized into 5 associations. They adopted a 5-year project for using new approaches for evangelism among the Pwo Karens, who had been much slower to respond to the Gospel than the Sgaw Karens. I was interested to meet a young Japanese couple who had just finished seminary and believed the Lord was calling them to work with the Karens. In order to find out if they could be used, they came for the TKBC annual meeting, and were then invited back to teach at the Bible school at the Center for the Uplift- of the Hill Tribes. Later I received a letter from them in California, where they were taking a course to improve their English. It was good that Asians are responding more and more to the call for foreign missionary service, but often their churches were unable to support them overseas. So, we in the West continued to need to provide some financial support even though the number of missionaries we sent out was decreasing.

April 11-26, I took a holiday and returned to Sangkla where I had worked for 22 years. I attended the annual association meeting of the 16th Phak (Gethsemane Association), and it was good to see many friends and former co-workers again. I was pleased to see from the reports of the churches that the amount of income received from tithes had increased. In 3 churches it was then about 5 times more than 2 years before when I retired. The total membership of the 6 churches and 3 branch churches was reported as 525. (It was somewhere between 400-500 when I left 2 years before.) Four of the churches had a regular evangelistic outreach in villages several hours away from them. A new evangelistic policy was adopted – from then on, no new evangelists or home mission workers would be hired by the association. Rather, the local churches would do the hiring, supervising, and encouraging and the salaries would be split half and half – the association matching the funds raised by the local churches. All was not rosy, however, as one branch church was threatened with a split because of personality conflicts.

A local girl named Naw Tapee just graduated from Bible School and came back to work full-time with the association Women's Society. They could not give her a very large cash salary; but she would spend several months in turn at each village where there was a Women's Society. She would encourage and help the women, and they would provide housing and food for her. The Church of Christ in Thailand (CCT) Women's Society made a grant to provide a travel allowance for her. As the women's work developed, and more income on the association level increased, the Association was able to support its own programs.

After the association meetings I travelled around to most of the 16th District Association's churches, in most cases being able to spend only one night at each place. The churches were spread out over an area roughly equivalent to the distance between Boston and New York City, so it usually took at least half a day to get from one to the next. By that time there were good roads to all but one. That one was on the far side of the big reservoir and was reached by motorboat.

The preparation of the basic language book took longer than I had anticipated, but the Language and Orientation Committee expressed satisfaction with what I had been able to accomplish and gave some helpful advice.

One big concern that we had in Maesariang was the need for doctors at the Christian Hospital there. It was registered as a 21-bed hospital and as such had to have 2 doctors and 5 nurses registered with the government. One of the 2 doctors returned to the USA for medical reasons, and it was not certain whether she would be able to return. Dr. Bina Sawyer carried on alone, which means she was on call 24 hours a day 7 days a week. It was almost impossible for foreign doctors to meet the requirements for registration, and Thai doctors usually didn't want to work in remote areas where they could not have a private practice on the side.

A very generous gift of $300 sent to me by check last month in August 1991. I took the liberty of donating it to the new AIDS Educations Project with which one of my colleagues in Thailand had become involved. She is a BIM. missionary named Kimberly Brown (Kim for short) and assigned to the Maesariang Christian Hospital. Then the Lord has put a burden on her heart to set up a project and train workers in the tribal program to teach about AIDS and how to prevent it. Many girls were being sold or tricked into prostitution, which unfortunately was big business in the country. The government finally acknowledged that there was a real problem in connection with AIDS. They tried to do what they could do to educate the public in Thai, but many of the tribal people knew little or no Thai, so they were glad that we started to do something in the tribal languages.

The government sent her copies of a bi-monthly report, and the last issue reported 32,000 confirmed HIV positive cases. The number in each 2-weeks' period increased by 500-600 on average each time, and the government estimated that there were really 10 times that number. Prostitution due both to the lifestyle of Thai men in general and to the promotion of tourism, as well as a growing number of drug users caused the disease to spread rapidly. With no known cure at that time, all HIV positive cases eventually developed AIDS. In Machongoorn Province (in which Maesariang is located) 50% of the confirmed cases were people from tribal groups. The Akha and Lahu in the Chiangmai Province had a larger percentage of girls sold or tricked into prostitution than the Karen tribe, but the number of Karens increased also. In one case of 3 sisters, they were all in high school but someone from the city came and offered the girls a good job for 1 month during their hot season vacation. They accepted the offer, only to find themselves in a den of slavery. Two of them escaped by jumping out of a window, one of them breaking her back in the process. Of the 3 sisters, one died of AIDS and the other 2 were HIV positive. Girls were kidnapped, tricked, or sometimes sold by poor uneducated families who needed money and didn't realize what would happen to their daughters. The crime suppression police department was raiding brothels from time to time, and often the tribal girls who had been prostitutes were sent to one of our New Life Center (Lauren Bethel was in charge of) in Chiangmai. The girls all told of being beaten many times if they didn't cooperate, sometimes so hard that they lost consciousness. One 13-year-old girl was beaten badly, then raped by 50 different men in one night. So, you can see why it was important to start a campaign to warn the villages so that they wouldn't let their children go away unless with someone they knew and trusted. Also, the need for educating children and young people, especially those who planned to go to middle school or high school in the towns, of the dangers of AIDS and how to prevent getting it.

Both Canadian and Australian groups showed an interest in funding the project. Encouraged by the former group Kim started on faith. The Lord provided an Akha man and a Karen nurse who were willing to work full time and a Lahu woman who gave some time. At one point they prepared literature in the languages of the people. Kim and the Karen nurse made presentations to a number of groups of students, Christians, church leaders, and missionaries. Near Maesariang town an office was rented and fixed up and in Chiangmai also. The way the Lord had been leading and working things out, it seemed as though that was of the Lord.

The language and Orientation Committee decided that phonetics should not be used in the books since Karen script is comparatively easy to learn to read and write; rather, some introductory lessons should be prepared teaching the script as well as pronunciation drills for sounds which didn't occur in English. So, by the beginning of November I had completed a set of 8 lessons for those purposes. I had also revised Book I quite a bit.

I was very happy that Alice Shae, a BIM missionary who worked in Sabah, Malaysia, came to visit Bina Sawyer and me for several days prior to the annual missionary conference at the end of July 1991. (Her husband went somewhere else in north Thailand at the same time in order to carry out an obligation.) Alice, Bina, and I had known each other since our days in Burma as missionaries.

The annual missionary conference at our mission cottages down on the shore of the Gulf of Thailand had a smaller attendance than usual because a larger number of missionaries were home on furlough. However, it was a time of blessing physically, mentally, socially, and spiritually.

A 4-day leadership training institute in one of the Karen villages was held in July. The rainy season hadn't ended, so there were only 16 from other villages besides those who were to teach. But quite a number of the local Christians attended, so in the end there was a good number and a good response. The Maesariang Association tried to have such institutes 3 times a year, each time in a different village so that local villagers could have a chance to participate and leaders from all of the churches in the association might get further training. Those from elsewhere arrived on a Saturday, shared responsibility in the various Sunday services, then had worship and training sessions for 3 days. I was asked to teach about the responsibilities of church leaders – a subject I didn't feel that I had a very good background for teaching. But the Lord guided in such a way that the sessions were a blessing even though the subject may not have been dealt with quit3 the way expected. The villagers were quite poor but very hospitable and very appreciative of our coming to give them instruction and encouragement and to have fellowship with them.

Two great concerns:

1. Economic refugees from Burma. A large number of Karens and Mons came across the border from Burma into Thailand during the previous 30 years because living conditions in Burma were so difficult. Those who settled down in Thailand for more than 15 years had been given refugee identification cards and were allowed to live and work within the district where they were located, although if they worked for an institution or company, they had to get a work permit. Then suddenly, under the military government which took over the country early that year all the Karens were being forced to move into camps near the border, where there was very little likelihood that they would be allowed to farm or earn their own living. It affected a number of our churches as well as the KRCH hospital staff and patients. Also, the national evangelists working with the Telakhon were included; so, a lot of the work of the 16th district Association was in a very uncertain state.

2. The AIDS Education Project. In a letter to the editor of the Bangkok Post dated September 28, 1991, Dr. Malcolm Potts of London, who for the previous 5 years had been responsible for a multinational team working in AIDS prevention in 40 countries, wrote: "The harsh reality is that AIDS has taken off more rapidly in Thailand than in practically any other country. In 4 years,

Thailand was thought to have accumulated approximately half as many cases of AIDS virus infection as the USA and Thailand had well over 4 times as many Aids infected people) accumulated in over just 10 years' history of the epidemic... From the point of view of Thailand and in particular the nightlife of Bangkok, all the evidence was that people were at extremely high risk. In fact, more Thais were condemned to die from the disease than people were killed by the 2 atomic bombs dropped on Japan at the end of World War II."

According to Dr. Saisuree Chutikul, the lone female cabinet minister in Thailand, prostitutes were under mafia influence. She wrote that she had heard unofficially that they exercised great influence over high-ranking police officials. She said that the low-ranking local policemen were quite aware of all prostitution dens, but they were too intimidated to take notice. More and more tribal girls 13 years and up were being bought, tricked, or kidnapped and forced into prostitution. Not only did many tourists come for that sort of entertainment, but also the Thai man's lifestyle was such that promiscuity had become a social norm. This plus the increase in the use of heroin was resulting in the rapid spread of the AIDS virus. The government as well as a number of other organizations were taking steps to provide education of the public concerning the danger and prevention of AIDS. However, they didn't have anyone who knew the tribal languages and so they couldn't do anything for those people. So, the Christian Hospital in Maesariang set up a project with Kim Brown and a Karen nurse counterpart in charge, to provide education to the Karen, Lahu, and Akha tribes on the village level. The Lord raised up a well-trained Akha man and a Lahu woman who were concerned and wanted to work with this project. An office was set up; also, the preparation of flip charts and leaflets for disseminating information were prepared. Since we already had Christian work among these 3 tribes, we had contacts in a number of their villages.

The AIDS education project for tribal people moved forward. Additional workers were taken on and were trained, pamphlets in the 3 languages were prepared, surveys were made in many villages. Flip charts were pre-tested and where pictures didn't convey the intended meaning to the villagers, they were redone. AIDS education sessions were held in a fair number of villages 9 and cassettes were prepared.

My Work

As for me, from October 17-December 4, I took responsibility for overseeing the work in a Pwo Karen village about 5 km, from Maesariang town, while the German missionary who worked there, Gerda Meinusch, returned to Germany to be with a sister who had had a hip replacement. Al though I continued to work on the Sgaw Karen language lessons while there, I also made some progress in learning their dialect of Pwo Karen, which was different from what I had learned in Kanburi and Burma.

I had hoped to attend the 75th anniversary of the Karen Baptist Convention in Burma December 29-31, Then Sue Powers, one of our Baptist missionaries in Bengal-Orissa, invited me to attend their South Asia Missionary Fellowship conference January 2-6 and then visit her in Balasore, I decided to do so also. In the end the Burma government didn't give permission for me to attend. But I went ahead to India anyway. It was good to fellowship with the Baptist missionaries (including Southern Baptist, Canadian Baptist, and Swedish Baptist) working in India, as well as several retirees back for a visit. Bob Roberts, who was in charge of World Mission Support at Valley Forge, gave us some unforgettable Bible Studies, and other Valley Forge staff gave us some encouraging news concerning plans to put more life into World Mission promotion. I was especially interested in the work Esther Wiebe had been doing among the gypsy women in the area, who were no longer itinerant and were very poor. The women were first drawn into the project to learn needlework as a source of supplementing their income. Then gradually they learned to read, and later to start studying the Bible. Another interesting project she had been involved in was a rehabilitation project for the elderly and for those who had disabilities. The elderly become substitute parents for the children with disabilities, all of whom lived in a community of cottages.

After the conference I went with Sue Powers to Balasore, Bengal-Orissa, a train trip taking almost 2 full days. It was good to visit Sue in her own home, and to become a hit acquainted with her co-workers and the

Christian work in the area. I was especially impressed with the program for the deaf integrated with the primary school. The deaf children were in a special class, where they were taught to produce intelligible sounds, to lip-read, as well as to read, write, and do arithmetic. I understood that they had 1-2 classes a day with the other primary school children. (I believe one was for drawing), and they also attended school assemblies. By the time they finished the 6th grade, they were able to attend high school with children who could hear.

Permission was given by the government for 5 trips to be made in 1992, and I joined a party leaving from Chiangmai on February 16th. We had to wait in a Karen village for 5 days before we were able to get elephants to carry our stuff. We also took turns riding the elephants. We had never gone this way before but had been told the trip could be made in one day. Well, it was a long day – from 7:30 a.m. to 10:30 p.m. – and we as well as the elephants were really tired. Ben Dickerson, who had come up from Sangkla with 2 Karens, had arrived the day before and saw to it that hot water was in the thermos waiting for us. We spent 6 days there, much of the time discussing various matters with the Telakhon (We now decided to spell their name as the Sgaw Karens do – Talako). They never said anything straight out, but they also talked around and around issues without being specific. Nothing spectacular happened on this trip, but we were able to encourage the one family which had believed and whom the other villagers were trying to discourage. The man Pa Dee Do was a bold witness for Christ and read and studied the Bible every day. But others started saying that he was crazy. In addition to encouraging him and his wife, definite plans were made to start teaching the children songs, Bible stories, and moral teaching. Most of the Talakhon still didn't see the light at all and 1 or 2 were openly antagonistic. Unless there was a lot of prayer for them and for the native evangelists, Satan was not going to release his hold of them.

Unfortunately, shortly after I reached the village where we waited for the elephants, I became aware that I had developed dysentery. I had no medication and could only try to eat a non-roughage diet and stick it out till the end of the trip, but day by day I had less and less appetite and less and less energy. Then the last 2 days there, I began having fever in the afternoon. The day after I got back to Chiangmai (March 1st), a friend took me to the hospital, where I was admitted. It was discovered that I had developed a liver abscess, and I was in the hospital for 17 days. I got back to Maesariang and was getting stronger every day. I was very thankful for Christian hospitals, modern equipment, and for Christian friends who visited me and upheld me.

I decided to remain in Thailand until May 1993, when Dr. Bina Sawyer, with whom I was living, left Thailand to retire.

The 75th anniversary celebration of the Karen Baptist Convention (Burma), which had been postponed was held in Maymyo (north of Mandalay) December 24 – 27, 1992.

The AIDS Education Project for the Hill Tribes received a large grant from WHO sufficient to pay for salaries and preparation of educational materials for one year; so that was the cause for praise and rejoicing. The project was given the official name of Health Project for Tribal People, and the new office building was officially dedicated on July 1st, 1992.

New office and part of staff of Health

Dr. Bina Sawyer, with whom I had been living, had a stroke affecting her right side on July 27, 1992. By God's grace and as the result of many prayers, she improved considerably. She didn't need to use a cane in the house and could write slowly. The therapist thought that she was.

able to stop her therapy temporarily in order to return to Thailand in May 1993, in order to dispose of her belongings. Kim Brown and Bina left the country, visited friends and former co-workers, and saw some of the other BIM work in Thailand, in the hope of doing some deputation later on. She officially retired as of May 1st.

On September 1, 1992, a choir group composed of about 30 Karens, including leaders of the Karen Baptist Convention as well as Bible school students from the Center for the Uplift of the Hill Tribes went to England for a 6- week tour of the churches beginning with the centennial celebration of the Baptist Missionary Society. They were well received everywhere as they sang and shared some of their culture and testimonies with folks there, and it was unforgettable experience for most of them.

The Family Life Center celebrated its 5th anniversary on November 1st, 1992, with a special program including the dedication of House No. 3. The Aids education project completed the printing of 40,000 colored posters (2 kinds in each of 4 languages—Sgaw Karen, Pwo Karen, Akha, and Lahu), 400 sets of flip charts (1 for each of the 4 languages), and 25,000 copies of a pamphlet explaining about the disease and its prevention. The teams gave teaching in many tribal villages and started holding training institutes for key village leaders (pastors, teachers, etc.) so that they could use the flip charts and teach in many more villages than the team members could reach. Neither the New Life Center nor the Aids project were able to find any dependable source of continuing funds, since most organizations gave grants for one year or less at a time, and so new funds had to be sought each year. Yet the work of both projects was increasingly important, as the number of HIV-positive and full-blown AIDS cases continues to increase rapidly in Thailand. So, please pray that the Lord will provide the right amount of funds at the right time from the right sources according to His perfect plan.

The big happening for me was the chance to attend the 75th Jubilee celebration of the Kayin Baptist Convention held at Pyin-Oo-Lwin (formerly Maymyo) in Myanmar (Burma) December 24-27. Although I didn't know until December 9th that I would be granted a visa, everything worked out so that I could be in Burma from the 22nd to the 31st, attend the celebrations, and visit many friends. I was able to visit whomever I wanted to, but Thra Clifford Kyaw Dwe the KBC General secretary, had to guarantee that I would not engage in any political activities. The theme of the convention was "Thank God and Go Forward." The main convention sermon was preached by Dr. Chit Maung. Thra Clifford was honored for his 32 years of service as KBC general secretary, and a number of full-time Christian workers with 40 years or more of service were also honored. Thra Clifford then officially turned responsibility over to the new general secretary, Thra Cooler. Two pastors were also ordained during the celebrations. It was estimated that about 3000 persons attended.

JUBILEE CELEBRATION

Maymyo, Burma – December 24 – 27, 1992

Worship Service

Dr. Clifford Kyaw Dwe
was honored for 32 years'
service as General Secretary

Convention theme: "Thank God and Go Forward"

75ᵀᴴ JUBILEE WORSHIP SERVICE – DECEMBER 27, 1992

Ko Tha Byu Bible School Choir

3 bands combined play at main Jubilee worship service

Ordination of 2 pastors during the celebration

Conclusion

I arranged to join the "Greece and Turkey Tour" sponsored by Eastern Baptist Theological Seminary in Thessaloniki on June 1st. We spent 8 days visiting places where Paul the Apostle travelled and ministered, including a 3-day cruise. The big attraction for me is that Dr. Manfred Brauch, president of EBTS, was the tour leader. Following the tour, I visited friends on the east coast before continuing on to California.

While waiting for accommodations to become available for me to become a resident at Pilgrim Place, a retirement community in Claremont, California, for full-time Christian workers. The Lord has worked things out for me to sublet Elizabeth Chambers' apartment in that very retirement community while she is in the Philippines for 10 months.

I left Thailand the night of May 31, 1993, and joined the Greece and Turkey Tour in Thessaloniki, Greece, in the late afternoon of the 1st of June. The tour leader was Dr. Manfred T. Brauch, president of Eastern Baptist Theological Seminary, included visits to a number of cities where Paul preached as well as 3-day cruise on the Aegean Sea.

We arrived in Philadelphia the evening of June 9th, and I stayed in the area for 3 nights, staying with a different friend each night, and did a bit of business during the day. Then I visited friends and relatives in Hyattsville, MD., and Washington, D.C., for about a week, after which I visited my sister and brother-in-law in Montrose, CO, for several days before going on to Claremont.

The prime minister's office has praised this project as being the best of its kind in the country. Furthermore, the project was invited to present a paper at an international conference on Aids in Germany in early June. Margaret, a Lahu nurse on the staff, presented the paper, and she and Kimberly Brown set up a poster display and were on hand to answer the questions. This was a very great honor resulted in many more contacts, ideas, and/or funds.

As for the New Life Center, the needed funds for next year were granted. 15 girls from this project spent 4 ½ months in the USA beginning June 1st on a choir tour, including some testimonies and talking about the project. They attended the Biennial Convention, ABW (American Baptist

Women), and World Missions conferences at Green Lake. In between, they sang in many churches in the west and Midwest.

Another answer to prayer was that Bina Sawyer got back in Thailand, arriving April 30, and was busy sorting and disposing of her things. She looked like her former self except for being a little thinner (which she wanted to be), and she felt fine as far as her health was concerned. She could do most things for herself, albeit a bit slower; but the heat and humidity were quite a contrast from the weather in Maine (snow the day before she left), so that, plus fact that she kept going nearly all day long, had resulted in her feeling a bit tired in the evenings. However, the next morning found her ready to start in again. She got physical therapy at the McCormick Hospital in Chiangmai once every two weeks, and she did exercise every day. She got back home the first week of July.

I was planning to attend the annual meeting of the 16th District association of the Church of Christ in Thailand (the former Kwai River Christian Mission with which I worked) on April 3 – 7, as it was to be held in Bongti Village only about 3 hours' drive away from Bangkok. As it turned out, I was asked to lead the Sgaw Karen Bible study, while Acharn Prakai, vice moderator of the CCT, led the Bible study in Thai. The Tanaosri Church dedicated its new building and formally established its new pastor on the 4th. In addition to the Bible studies, devotional periods, and business sessions during the meetings, in the evenings there were choir, quartette, and solo competitions, as well as Bible recitation contests – 1 for children up to 12 years and 1 for those over 12. In the late afternoons there were also volleyball competitions; so, there was a festival atmosphere at the meetings.

I was happy to have Thra Honor Nyo visit me in April for a week on his way back to Burma from the Philippines. He had completed all of his classwork but had to return to Burma to do research in preparation for his thesis. He got to visit Chiangmai and Maesariang as well as Bangkok and saw some persons he already knew, made some new friends, and learned something about the work among the Karens of Thailand. He expected to return to his former position of general secretary of the Bassein-Myaungmya Sgaw Karen Association, composed of more than 200 churches.

Printed in the United States
by Baker & Taylor Publisher Services